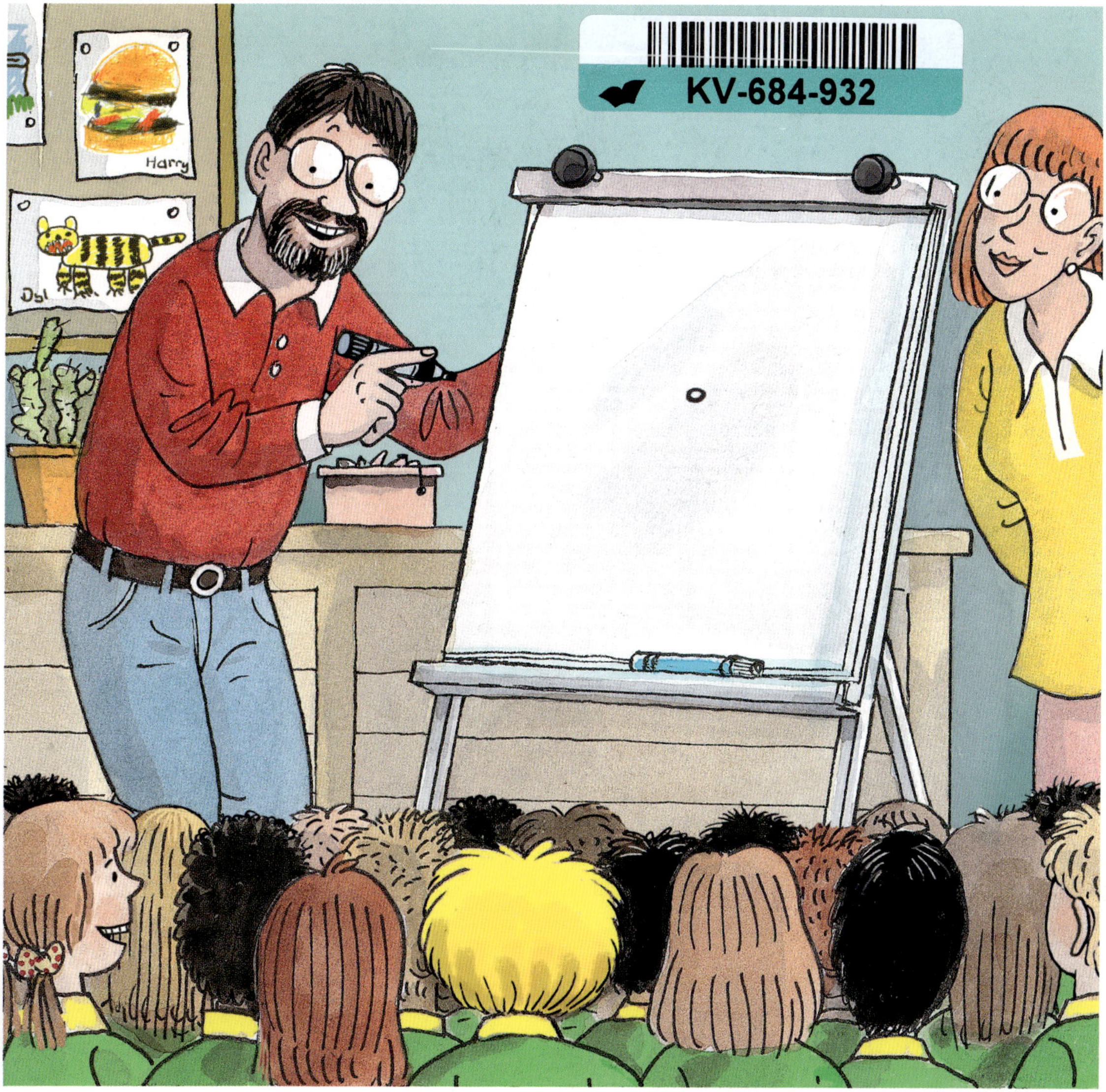

The man had a big pad.

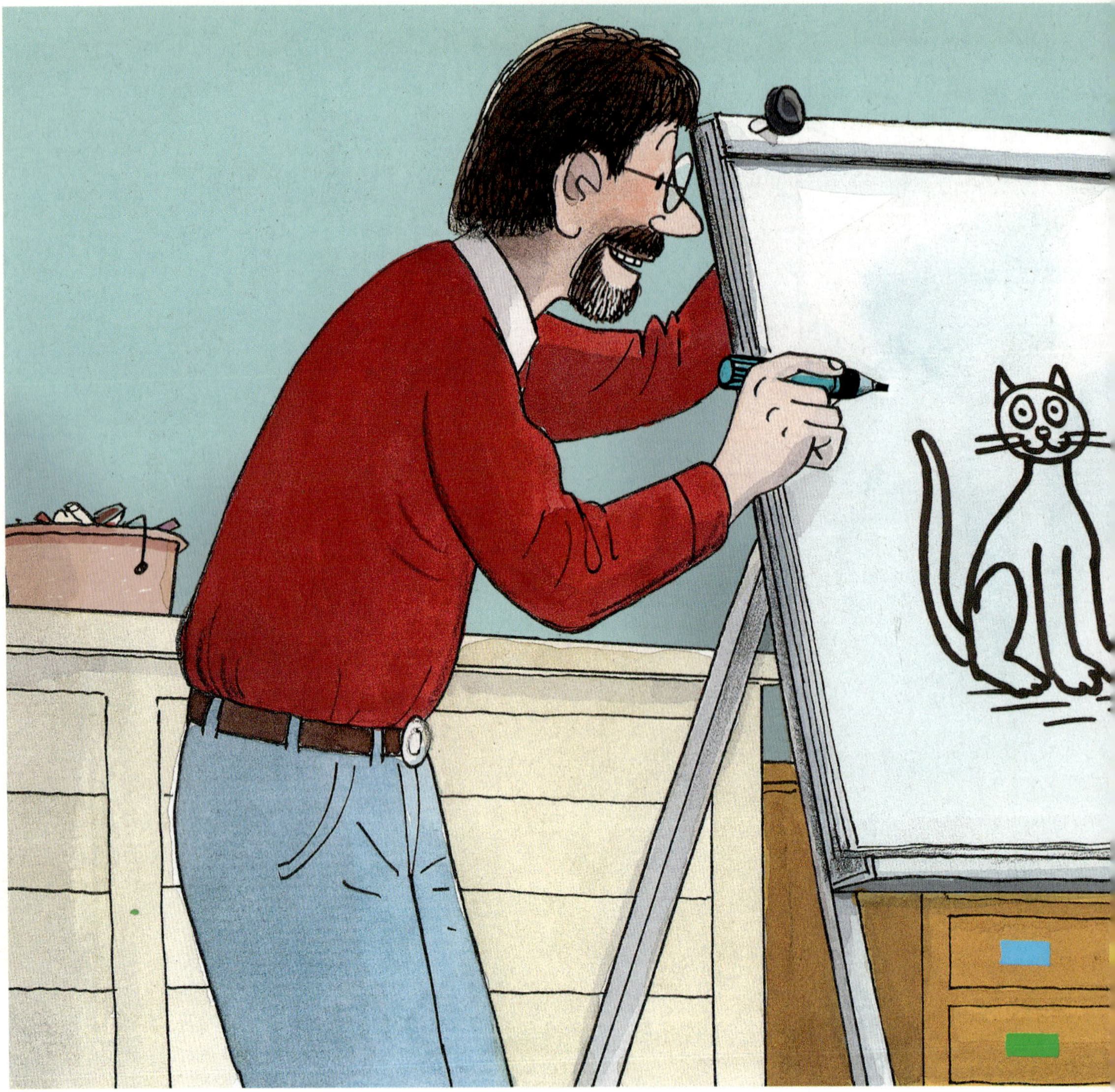

He had a pen.

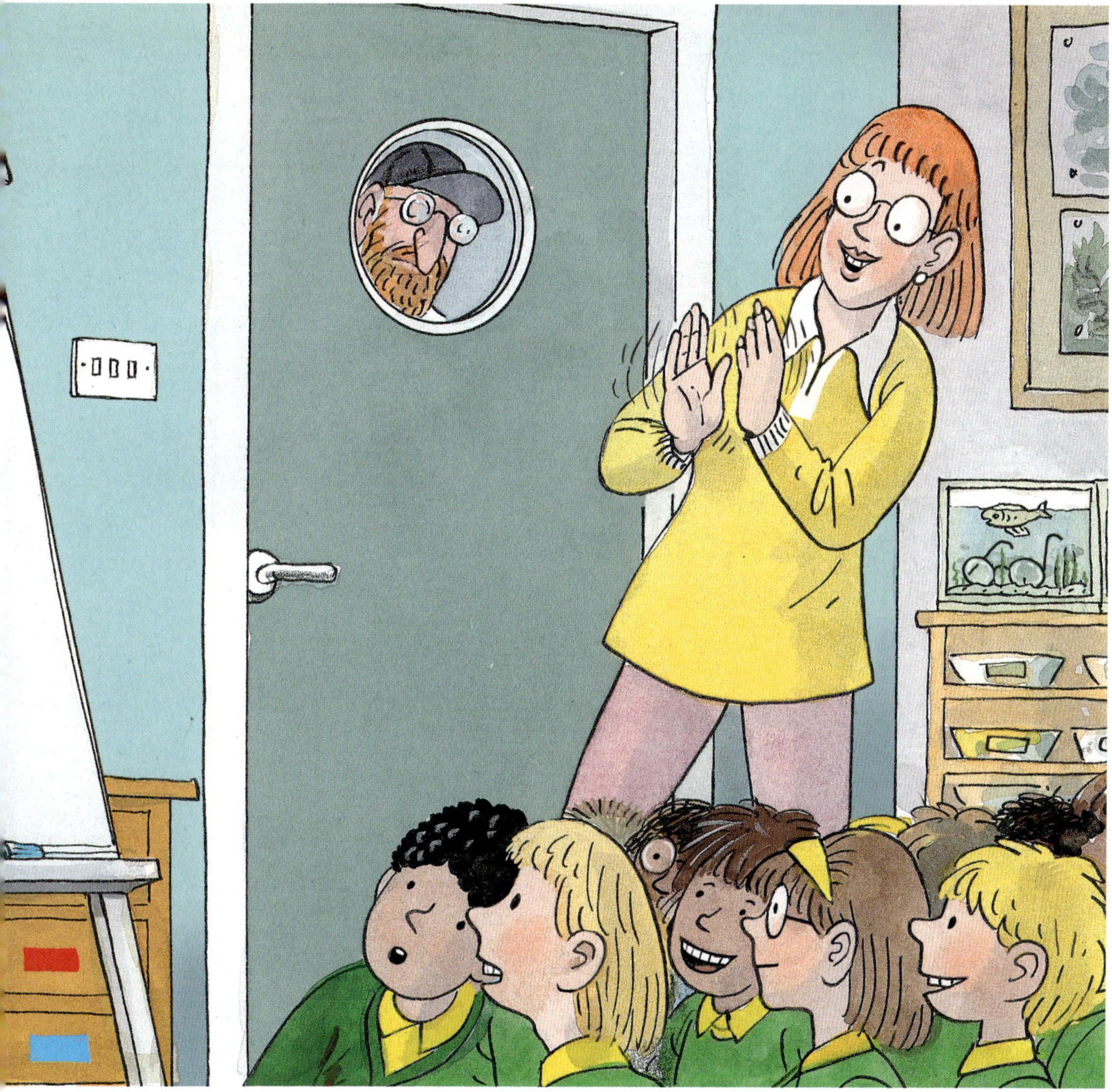

He did a picture of a cat.

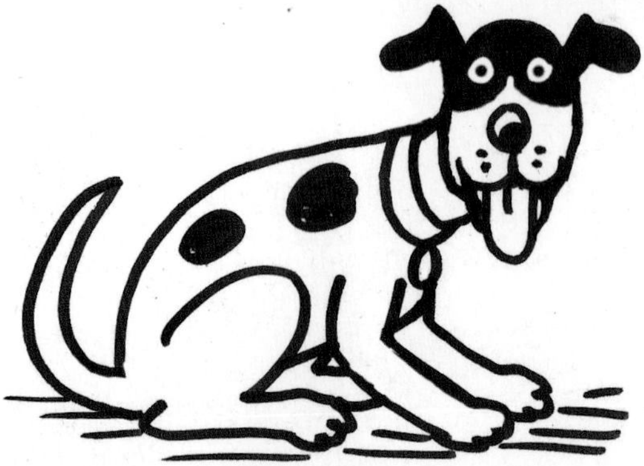

He did a picture
of a dog.

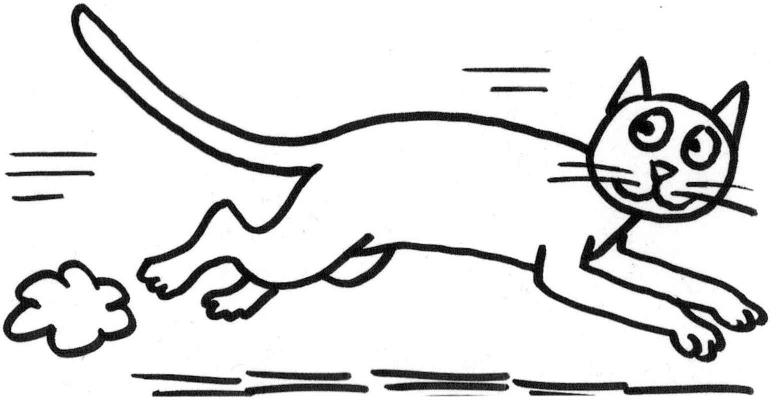

The cat ran.

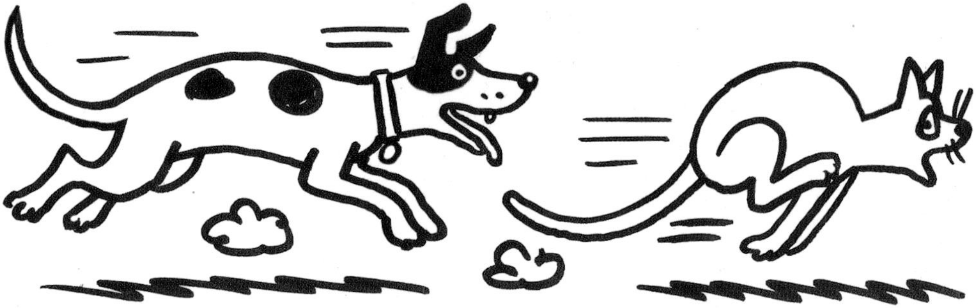

The dog ran.

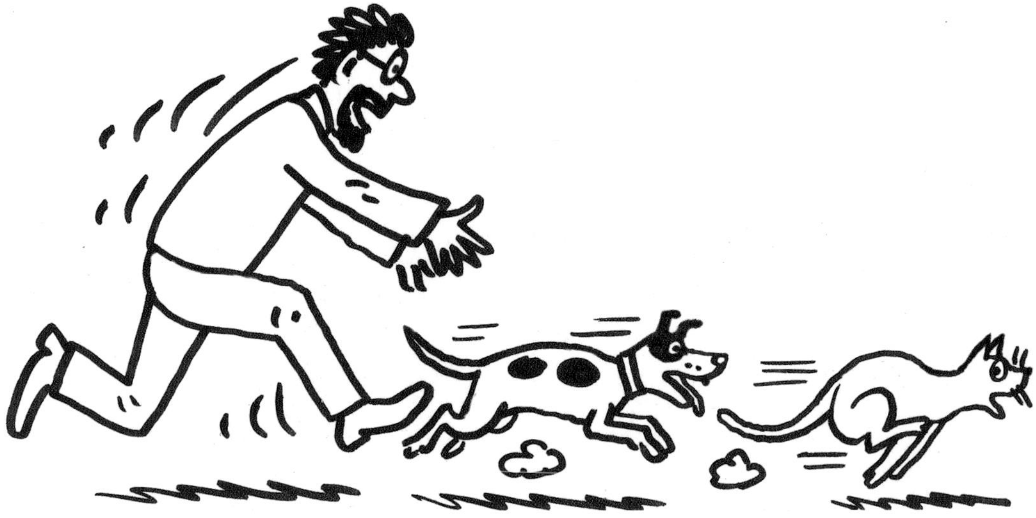

The man ran.

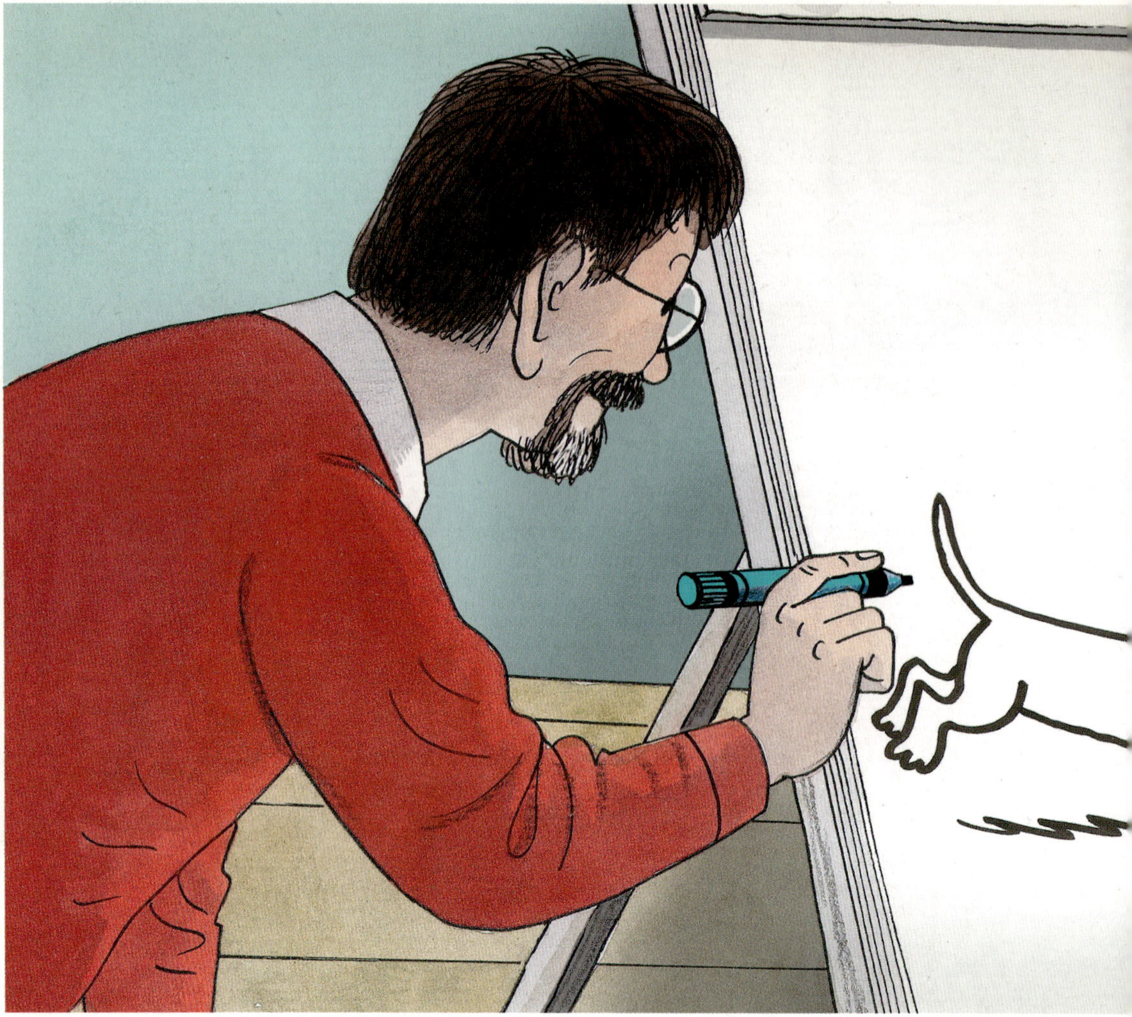

He did a picture of
a long dog.

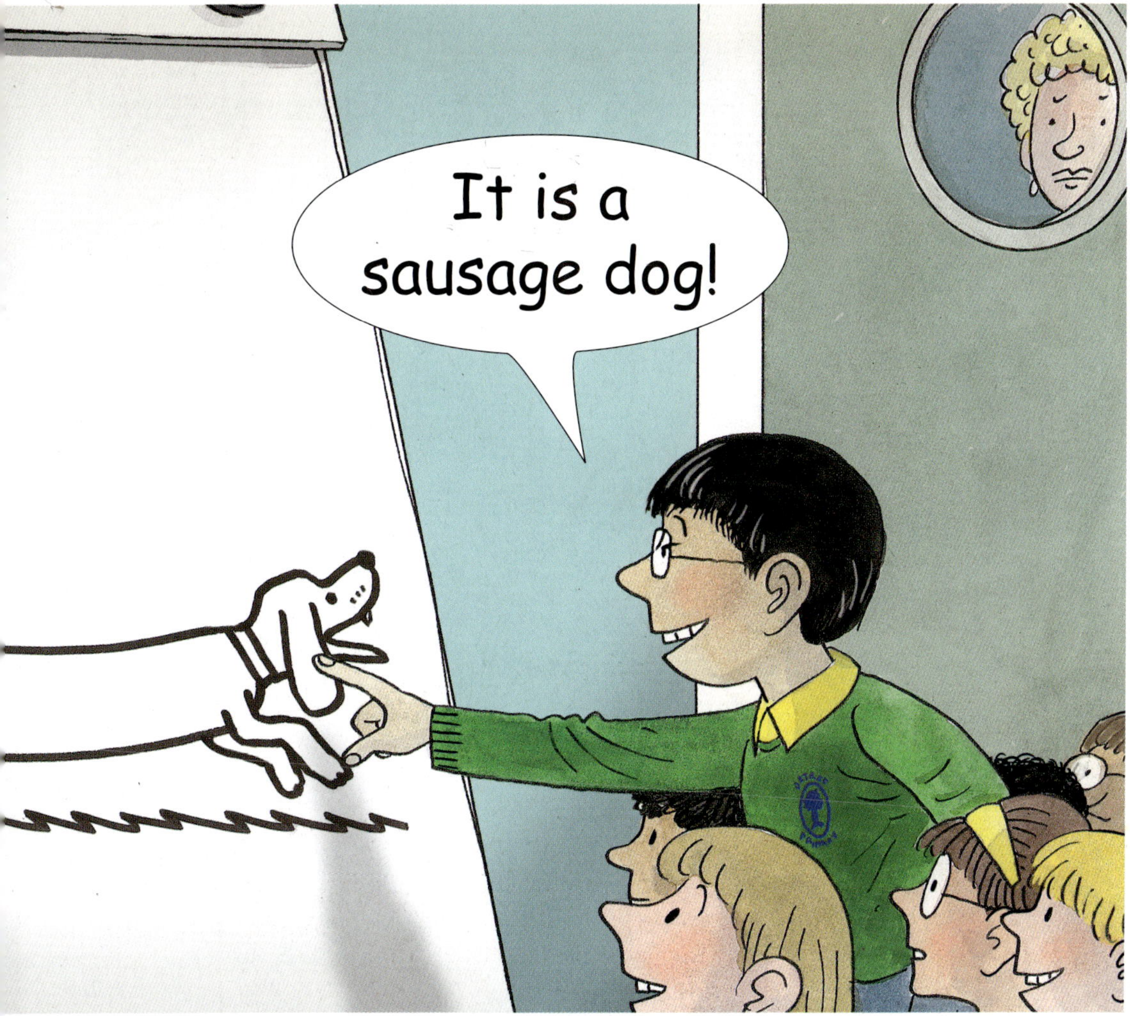
It is a sausage dog!

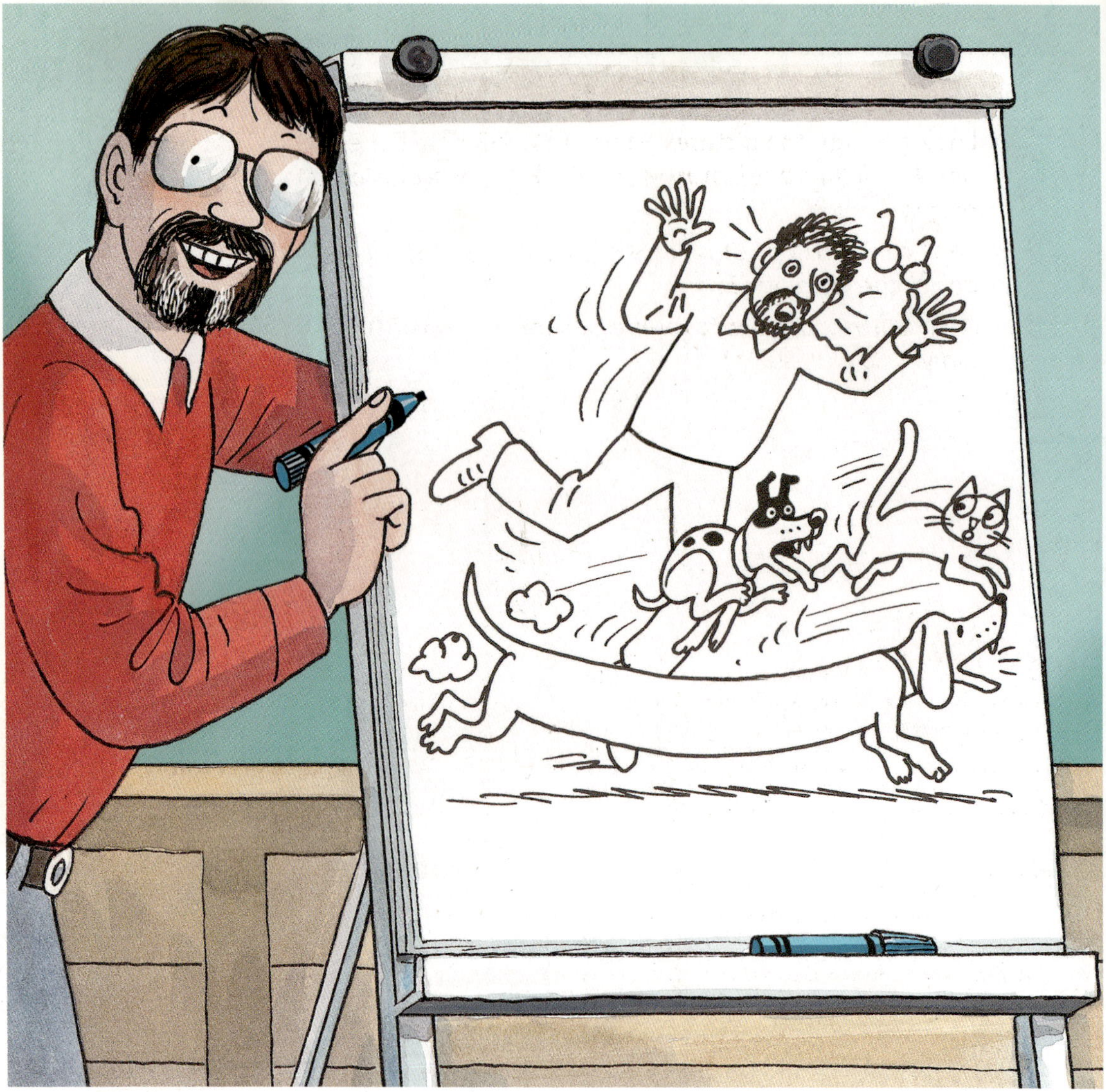

The picture man was fun.